ANIMAL LIVES
The Rabbit

KINGFISHER
Larousse Kingfisher Chambers Inc.
95 Madison Avenue
New York, New York 10016

First published in 2000
2 4 6 8 10 9 7 5 3 1
1TR/0100/SC/RPR(RPR)/150NYM

LIBRARY OF CONGRESS CATALOGING-IN-PUBLICATION DATA
has been applied for.

Series editor: Miranda Smith
Series designer: Sarah Goodwin

ISBN 0-7534-5214-6

Printed in Hong Kong

ANIMAL LIVES
The Rabbit

Illustrated by
Bert Kitchen

Written by
Sally Tagholm

KINGFISHER

NEW YORK

The farmer has gone home, and the rabbits have the field to themselves. The brown buck sits on guard, his long, battle-scarred ears picking up the tiniest sound. His big eyes scan the meadow; his nose trembles and twitches in the evening air. The rabbits have not strayed far from home. They graze peacefully in the sweet grass, sprinkled with clover and daisies.

 **S**uddenly the spell is broken. Danger looms as a buzzard circles high above, his piercing eyes searching the field for his supper. The buck sounds the alarm with a heavy thump of his strong back legs. As one, the rabbits freeze, then turn and race for cover, pounding across the smooth, green turf at top speed. The hungry bird plummets down, claws outstretched. Too late. The speedy bunnies reach home just in time, diving down the grassy holes that lead into their sandy warren, safe and sound.

he maze of tunnels and burrows stretches far into the side of the hill, with plenty of room for the entire colony of rabbits. There are several secret entrances and exits, as well as some special holes in case of emergency. These holes are just big enough for rabbits to squeeze through, but too small for most predators.

After nibbling all those tender green plants, the rabbits produce their first droppings—soft, round pellets of only half-digested food. There is still plenty of nourishment in them, so the rabbits tuck in again and swallow them whole, enjoying a second meal. Tomorrow, when they venture out again, they will leave their final droppings above ground, dry and hard, like little heaps of smooth, black peppercorns.

When it is time to feed outside again, the buck peers cautiously from the shadowy mouth of the warren, checking that the coast is clear. Only then do the young rabbits and does hop out into the fresh spring air. The buck is especially wary—and not just of predators. It is the breeding season, and there may be other males on the prowl, waiting to challenge him over one of his does. He marks out his territory to warn his rivals, rubbing his chin against plants and twigs and sliding it along the ground, leaving a strong scent trail.

**A**lthough he has already fathered several different litters this spring, the buck is ready to mate again. He chooses a young doe, dancing around her to see if she is interested. At first, she hesitates, not quite sure. Then, with a quick flick of her little white tail, she joins in the game. They chase each other around and around, this way and that, lolloping and leaping through the long grass.

It is not long before the complicated game is over. The rabbits sniff each other, their noses twitching, ready to mate. They are quite safe—there are no rival males around, and the rest of the rabbits are grazing safely in the next field. The doe gives the signal, crouching down low on her belly and lifting her hindquarters into the air. The buck climbs onto her to mate. Afterward he topples over, roly-poly, onto the ground beside her. They rest quietly, side by side, a soft, brownish-gray bundle in the long, green grass. From time to time, the buck gently licks the doe, his pink tongue tenderly preening her face and ears. They doze peacefully together, warming themselves in the late spring sun.

he doe starts to work on her nest, just outside the main warren. She digs down, her front paws flinging out a stream of sandy soil under her belly. It is hard work, and as she digs deeper and deeper, she has to turn and push the earth out with her chest. She makes the nest as comfortable as possible, lining it with a mattress of old leaves and grass and patches of velvety, green moss. She even pulls tufts of short, gray fur from her belly to make a soft, warm bed.

When they are born, four weeks later, the babies are hairless and cannot yet see or hear. They sleep quietly in their safe, dark nest, cocooned from the outside world. Each night the doe feeds her litter, then slips off into the darkness. She scratches the earth behind her, camouflaging the entrance to hide it from hungry badgers, foxes, and weasels. The babies grow quickly now. In only a week, they have developed fine, soft fur and tiny claws and teeth. By now, they can hear one another's squeaks. Very soon their bright, brown eyes will open.

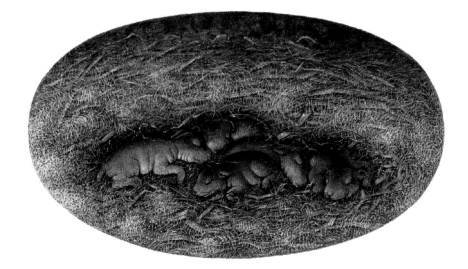

B y the time they are three weeks old, it is getting crowded in the nest, and the growing brood is ready to investigate the world above ground. The doe stands guard as the five young rabbits timidly peek out of the burrow for the first time, then hop, one by one, into the sweet, fresh air. Safe under their mother's anxious gaze, they explore the field, playing and nibbling the grass.

The rabbits often come out to feed at night, when the darkness helps hide them from animals on the prowl. Sometimes, they hop right around the farm to the vegetable garden, where there are neat rows of baby lettuce, carrots, and peas. But they must always be on guard, and they stay very near the burrow when the moon is bright. They are just the right size for the old barn owl who lives in the woods and swoops silently over the fields looking for juicy morsels. The doe stays close to her young, guarding them well and teaching them to be alert to the slightest sign of danger. Soon, she will have to leave them to fend for themselves. She has mated again, and must start work on a nest for her next litter of babies.

The five young rabbits have to be careful now that they are on their own. An army of predators lurks in the bushes and fields. The rabbits are especially wary of the big, brown fox who slinks through the farmyard and frightens the hens. He is hungry, and the sight of so many plump young rabbits tempts him out into the fields. Stealthily, he creeps closer, keeping low to the ground, but the rabbits are too quick. With a thump on the ground, they raise their white tails in the air, signaling danger to one another, then bolt for cover.

**A**ll five rabbits are strong and healthy, and despite the many dangers, they should survive. Before the end of the summer, the young does might even have babies of their own, and the warren will spread its maze of tunnels and burrows deeper into the side of the hill. Soon, the young bucks will be ready to set off and explore. One day, they will probably start colonies of their own.

THE RABBIT

Scientific name: *Oryctolagus cuniculus* (European rabbit)

Nickname: Bunny.

Size: Adults measure up to 15.5 inches from head to tail.

Weight: Up to 4.5 pounds.

Distribution: Europe, Australia, New Zealand, North and South America, Africa, Asia.

Habitat: Grassland, woodlands, cultivated fields, sand dunes, marshes, mountains, moors, cliffs.

Food: Grass, clover, sorrel, daisies, roots, crops, young trees, garden vegetables. Rabbits can eat one pound of fresh green food daily.

Breeding: One buck (male rabbit) mates with several does (female rabbits). Litters of 2 to 8 kittens (rabbit babies) are produced at monthly intervals, mainly between April and September.

Predators: Eagles, hawks, owls, ravens, crows, buzzards, black-backed gulls, coyotes, foxes, badgers, ermine, weasels, ferrets, dogs, cats, humans.

Relatives: Snowshoe rabbit (an American hare), pygmy rabbit, bristly rabbit, Mexican volcano rabbit, brown hare, antelope hare, Cape hare, cottontail (in North and South America), Blue Alpine or mountain hare, woolly hare, red rock hare, Riu-Kiu hare.

HISTORY OF THE WILD RABBIT

European, or Old World, rabbits were originally found only in northwest Africa, Spain, and Portugal. A valuable source of meat and fur, they were introduced to most of the rest of Europe about 800 years ago. Much later, they were taken to other parts of the world such as Australia, New Zealand, and North and South America. Over the years, some of these domestic rabbits escaped into the wild, and with their astonishing rate of breeding, soon became a pest to farmers. Cottontails are New World (*Sylvilagus*) rabbits, and are now commonly found in the wild in Canada, the United States, and Mexico. They take the name cottontail from their tufty, white tails, which look like little balls of cotton.

HOW TO WATCH WILD RABBITS

Rabbits are most active at night, so watch for them in a grassy field at dusk. Look carefully for clues: rabbit tracks, small tufts of fur, or gnawed tree bark are signs that a rabbit has been there. Also look for small, round droppings, which are usually found near the burrow. To find out if a burrow is inhabited, gently lay some small sticks across the entrance; if a rabbit enters, the sticks will be disturbed. If you are lucky enough to see a rabbit, remember that they are easily frightened. Try to stay downwind of the animal, be very still while you are watching, and keep quiet as you move away.

RABBIT WORDS

buck male rabbit

burrow hole or tunnel dug by rabbits for shelter

camouflage to hide something by making it blend into the background

colony extended family of rabbits that lives in a warren

doe female rabbit

droppings round pellets of digested food

graze to eat grass

kitten a baby rabbit

litter a group of baby rabbits born at the same time from the same mother

predator animal that kills and eats other creatures

preening smoothing the fur

prey animal that is hunted for food

warren network of tunnels and burrows where a colony of rabbits lives

FOR FURTHER INFORMATION

International Wildlife Education and Conservation
237 Hill Street
Santa Monica, CA 90405
(310) 392 6257
www.iwec.org

World Wildlife Fund
1250 24th Street NW
Washington, D.C. 20037
(800) 225 5993
www.worldwildlife.org

National Association for Humane and Environmental Education
P.O. Box 362
East Haddam, CT 06423-0362
(860) 434 8666
www.nahee.org

House Rabbit Society
P.O. Box 1201
Alameda, CA 94501
(781) 643 0981
www.rabbit.org

INDEX

ACKNOWLEDGMENTS

The author and publishers thank Muriel Kitchen and John Tagholm for the photographs on the jacket.